NEWTON FREE LIB
330 HOMER ST.
NEWTON, MA 02459

W9-BRV-334

WITHDRAWN

# YOUR PASSPORT TO

# ETHIOPIA

by Ryan Gale

## CONTENT CONSULTANT

Semahagn Abebe, PhD
Assistant Professor
Arts and Sciences
Endicott College

CAPSTONE PRESS
a capstone imprint

Capstone Captivate is published by Capstone Press, an imprint of Capstone.
1710 Roe Crest Drive
North Mankato, Minnesota 56003
www.capstonepub.com

Copyright © 2021 by Capstone. All rights reserved. No part of this publication may be
reproduced in whole or in part, or stored in a retrieval system, or transmitted in any form
or by any means, electronic, mechanical, photocopying, recording, or otherwise, without
written permission of the publisher.

**Library of Congress Cataloging-in-Publication Data**
Names: Gale, Ryan, author.
Title: Your passport to Ethiopia / by Ryan Gale.
Description: North Mankato, Minnesota : Capstone Press, 2021. | Series:
    World passport | Includes index. | Audience: Grades 4-6
Identifiers: LCCN 2020001015 (print) | LCCN 2020001016 (ebook) | ISBN
    9781496684042 (hardcover) | ISBN 9781496687968 (paperback) | ISBN
    9781496684554 (pdf)
Subjects: LCSH: Ethiopia--Description and travel--Juvenile literature. |
    Ethiopia--Social life and customs--Juvenile literature.
Classification: LCC DT378.3 .G35 2021  (print) | LCC DT378.3  (ebook) | DDC
    916.304--dc23
LC record available at https://lccn.loc.gov/2020001015
LC ebook record available at https://lccn.loc.gov/2020001016

**Image Credits**
iStockphoto: CanY71, 20, DavorLovincic, 28, derejeb, 7, theasis, 27; Red Line Editorial: 5;
Shutterstock Images: Artush, 13, 17, AS Food studio, 22, G7 Stock, cover (flag), Gaulois_s,
cover (map), Giedriius, 16, Hailu Wudineh TSEGAYE, 10, John Wollwerth, 25, Marisha_SL,
6, Martchan, 19, RudiErnst, cover (bottom), Sarine Arslanian, 21, Simone Migliaro, 9,
zlikovec, 14
Design Elements: iStockphoto, Shutterstock Images

**Editorial Credits**
Editor: Jamie Hudalla; Designer: Colleen McLaren

All internet sites appearing in back matter were available and accurate
when this book was sent to press.

Printed in the United States of America.
PA117

# CONTENTS

CHAPTER ONE
## WELCOME TO ETHIOPIA! ...................................... 4

CHAPTER TWO
## HISTORY OF ETHIOPIA................................... 8

CHAPTER THREE
## EXPLORE ETHIOPIA ............................... 12

CHAPTER FOUR
## DAILY LIFE ....................................... 18

CHAPTER FIVE
## HOLIDAYS AND CELEBRATIONS ...................... 24

CHAPTER SIX
## SPORTS AND RECREATION............................ 26

GLOSSARY ............................................. 30
READ MORE/INTERNET SITES........................ 3 1
INDEX ................................................. 32

Words in **bold** are in the glossary.

# CHAPTER ONE

# WELCOME TO ETHIOPIA!

Mist rises from the loud Blue Nile Falls in Ethiopia. Green **tropical** forest surrounds the waterfall. Monkeys and colorful birds chatter in the trees. Blue Nile is one of the largest waterfalls in Africa. It is also one of Ethiopia's most popular places to visit.

Ethiopia is a country in eastern Africa. It has a variety of landscapes. There are tropical forests, deserts, mountains, and volcanoes. People come to the country to visit its famous outdoor markets and historical sites. They can also explore many national parks. These parks allow people to see the country's birds and animals in the wild.

# MAP OF ETHIOPIA

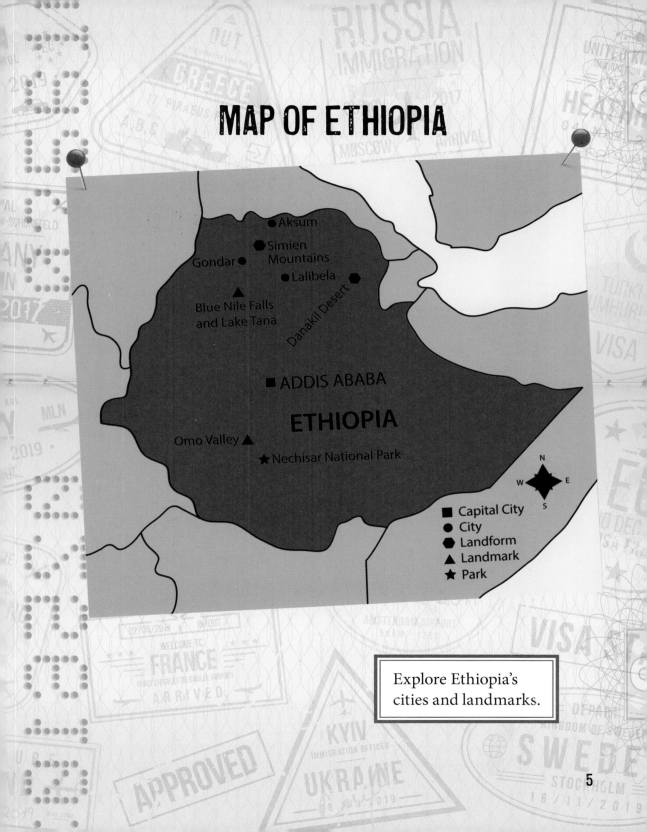

Aksum

Simien Mountains

Gondar

Lalibela

Blue Nile Falls and Lake Tana

Danakil Desert

■ ADDIS ABABA

ETHIOPIA

Omo Valley

★ Nechisar National Park

N
W   E
S

- ■ Capital City
- ● City
- ⬡ Landform
- ▲ Landmark
- ★ Park

Explore Ethiopia's cities and landmarks.

The Blue Nile Falls are in northern Ethiopia.

# PEOPLE OF ETHIOPIA

More than 108 million people live in Ethiopia. It is the second most populated country in Africa. Many people live in Addis Ababa. This is the capital city. It is at the base of Entoto Mountain in central Ethiopia. Ethiopia is home to many **native** groups. These include the Mursi and Surma. They live in small villages in the southern part of the country. **Tourists** visit these villages to learn about the peoples' **cultures**.

The capital city of Ethiopia is Addis Ababa.

# FACT FILE

**OFFICIAL NAME:** ...................................................... ETHIOPIA

**POPULATION:** ............................................................ 108,386,391

**LAND AREA:** ................................ 686,180 SQ. MI. (1,777,198 SQ KM)

**CAPITAL:** ............................................................... ADDIS ABABA

**MONEY:** .......................................................................... BIRR

**GOVERNMENT:** Parliamentary, with a prime minister as head of government and the president as head of state.

**LANGUAGE:** .............................................................. AMHARIC

**GEOGRAPHY:** Ethiopia is in eastern Africa. It is surrounded by land on all sides, sharing borders with Kenya, Sudan, Somalia, Djibouti, and Eritrea.

**NATURAL RESOURCES:** Ethiopia has valuable metals including platinum, gold, and copper. It also has natural gas and hydropower, which is energy taken from moving water.

# CHAPTER TWO

# HISTORY OF ETHIOPIA

People have lived in Ethiopia for millions of years. Scientists found very old human **fossils** there. They were more than two million years old! Ethiopia is in a land that was called Axum from 100 CE to around 900 CE. Axum traded with other countries. It became powerful. King Ezana was one of Axum's rulers. He became a Christian around 350 CE. The people of Axum worshipped many different gods before then. When Ezana became a Christian, many of his people did too. They started worshipping only one god.

Muslim people began moving to the region in the 600s CE. Muslims are followers of the religion Islam. Ethiopia still has many Christians and Muslims.

One of the oldest-known human skeletons is in the National Museum of Ethiopia. She is named Lucy.

In 2019, *Forbes* magazine listed President Sahle-Work Zewde as one of the world's 100 most powerful women.

# FIGHT FOR INDEPENDENCE

People from Europe began **colonizing** Africa in the 1800s. European cultures replaced many African cultures. Italy tried to colonize Ethiopia in the 1890s. Ethiopia's **emperor** and his people resisted. They fought Italy and won. Ethiopia stayed **independent**. It kept its unique cultures intact.

Italy and Ethiopia fought again in the 1930s. Ethiopia lost. Its emperor, Haile Selassie, fled the country. The Italian government did not treat the Ethiopian people fairly. In 1941, Selassie returned and freed his people from Italian rule.

# TIMELINE OF ETHIOPIAN HISTORY

**100 CE:** The kingdom of Axum forms.

**350s:** Christianity becomes one of Ethiopia's main religions.

**600s:** Muslims begin moving to Ethiopia.

**1889:** Addis Ababa becomes the capital of Ethiopia.

**1895–1896:** Ethiopians fight off an Italian invasion.

**1935:** Italy successfully invades Ethiopia.

**1941:** Ethiopia gains its independence from Italy.

**1974:** Selassie is removed from power, leading to civil war.

**1991:** Ethiopia removes its military-run government.

**2018:** Ethiopians elect their first female president.

An uprising broke out in Ethiopia in 1974. Many people did not want to be ruled by an emperor anymore. The people removed Selassie from power. This act led to a civil war.

Ethiopia declared a democratic government in the 1990s. The people run their own government in a form of democracy called a parliamentary government. In 2018, Ethiopians elected Sahle-Work Zewde as the country's first female president. Ethiopian presidents may stay in office for six years.

# CHAPTER THREE

# EXPLORE ETHIOPIA

Ethiopia has a landscape filled with natural wonders. The Blue Nile Falls is one of the country's most famous landmarks. The waterfall is 150 feet (46 meters) tall. It flows from the Blue Nile River.

The Blue Nile begins at Lake Tana in northern Ethiopia. Lake Tana is the country's largest lake. It has 37 islands. Many of them have old churches. Beautiful paintings fill the churches. Some emperors were buried on a few of the islands. Tourists can take boats to the islands and see their coffins.

Ethiopia is also known for its tropical forests. These forests are in the southwest part of the country. Fruits, vegetables, and coffee grow there.

Lake Tana is full of great white pelicans.

Geladas roam the Simien Mountains.

# MOUNTAINS AND DESERTS

The Simien Mountains are in northern Ethiopia. Ras Dashen Mountain is part of that mountain range. It is 14,872 feet (4,533 meters) tall. That makes it the highest mountain in the country. The Simien Mountains National Park is a popular place to hike and climb.

The Danakil Desert is in northeast Ethiopia. It is one of the hottest places on Earth. The temperature can reach as high as 130 degrees Fahrenheit (54.4 degrees Celsius). It gets very little rain. The desert contains large hot springs. These are warm pockets of water in the ground. Volcanoes also cover the landscape.

# WILDLIFE

Nechisar National Park is located in southwestern Ethiopia. It has a mix of grassy plains, hills, and forests. The park offers a great view of wildlife.

Ethiopia is home to many large animals such as zebras, giraffes, and elephants. These animals once roamed free in Ethiopia. Today, they mostly live in protected areas such as the Mago and Omo National Parks. Some animals can only be found in Ethiopia. These include the Ethiopian wolf, the baboon-like gelada, and the Bale monkey.

Ethiopia has more than 860 kinds of birds. Some native species include the Abyssinian woodpecker, the blue-winged goose, and the yellow-fronted parrot. Alligators are also common. They can be found in Ethiopia's lakes and rivers.

## FACT

The Erta Ale volcano in the Danakil Desert is one of the few volcanoes in the world with a pool of lava.

Ethiopia's national parks are full of rare animals, such as the Ethiopian wolf.

## DISCOVERING CITIES

Addis Ababa is packed with places to explore. The capital city is known for its many museums. People visit the Ethiopian National Museum and the Addis Ababa Museum. Tourists can learn about Ethiopian history through art and other **artifacts**. Famous churches, palaces, and marketplaces also line the streets.

Lalibela is in a mountainous region in northern Ethiopia. It has several churches carved out of rock. These churches are a UNESCO World Heritage Site.

The churches in Lalibela are cut from rock.

The city of Aksum was once the capital of the kingdom of Axum. Ancient people built large, carved stone pillars there. Some are still standing. Historians think they might mark the graves of ancient kings.

## MERCATO MARKET

The Mercato market is in Addis Ababa. It is the largest outdoor market in Africa. It covers several square miles. People sell clothing, food, and many other things. Many Ethiopians shop in markets like this throughout the country.

# CHAPTER FOUR

# DAILY LIFE

Many Ethiopians live and work in cities. Children are required to go to school between the ages of 7 and 16. Some children have to walk several miles to school. Children help with chores and play games when not at school. Some children work to help support their families. Many Ethiopians go to churches or mosques several times a week.

Other Ethiopians live in the countryside. They grow crops and raise animals for food. Some people sell their livestock for money.

## ETHIOPIAN GROUPS

Ethiopia has many groups of native people who live **traditional** lifestyles. Many live in small villages in the Omo Valley. This is in southwest Ethiopia. Some tribes have lived there for hundreds of years.

Children in Ethiopia start school at age 7.

In the countryside,
many people farm cattle.

The people of some Omo Valley tribes, such as the Mursi, live in wooden or grass huts. Many raise cattle for food. Others raise goats. People get water from a nearby river.

The Mursi live in the Omo Valley.

Each tribe has its own customs and traditions. The people of some native groups wear jewelry made of glass beads and shells. Some Mursi women wear disks in their lower lips. It is a sign of adulthood, though not all women choose to do so. Men and women may wear disks in their ears.

## FACT

Omo Valley is home to more than 70 different native groups.

Wat is Ethiopia's national dish. It's a type of stew.

## FOOD AND DRINK

Ethiopians enjoy a wide range of tasty foods. Farmers raise cows, chickens, lambs, and goats to eat. Many people do not have refrigerators to keep meat cold. They rub meat with spices to keep it from going bad. These spices also add flavor.

The national dish of Ethiopia is called wat. It is a type of stew. It is made with beef, chicken, or goat meat. It also has vegetables and spices.

Ethiopia is famous for its coffee. Ethiopians have been growing coffee beans for more than 1,000 years. Many people in the country drink coffee. It is also sold to other countries.

# BERBERE

*Berbere* is a mixture of spices. It is used to add flavor to many Ethiopian foods. With the help of a parent, you can make this recipe at home.

**Berbere Ingredients:**
- 1 cup red chili powder
- ½ cup paprika
- 1 tablespoon salt
- 1 teaspoon ground ginger
- 1 tsp onion powder
- 1 tsp ground cardamom
- ½ tsp garlic powder
- ¼ tsp ground cloves
- ¼ tsp ground cinnamon

**Berbere Directions:**

1. Mix all ingredients in a bowl.
2. Add to cooked beef, chicken, pork, or fish.

# CHAPTER FIVE

# HOLIDAYS AND CELEBRATIONS

Many Ethiopian festivals take place over several days and involve large feasts. One of these festivals is called Enkutatash, which celebrates the New Year in September. It also marks the end of the rainy season in Ethiopia. People buy new clothes, sing, dance, and give flowers to each other. Ethiopians celebrate their independence on Patriot's Day. This holiday began when Ethiopia gained its freedom from Italy in 1941.

## RELIGIOUS HOLIDAYS

Religious holidays are important to many Ethiopians. Christians celebrate Christmas and Easter. Many Christians in Ethiopia celebrate Orthodox Easter. This is in April or May. They attend a very long church service. Then they enjoy a meal.

During Enkutatash, people celebrate with singing and dancing in the streets.

Muslims participate in Ramadan. During this time, Muslims do not eat or drink from dawn until dusk every day for a month. They also recognize Eid al-Adha, remembering Abraham's obedience to God. Abraham is an important person in Islamic tradition.

**FACT**

Ethiopians prepare for Easter over a 55-day period. During this time, Christians do not eat meat or dairy products.

# CHAPTER SIX

# SPORTS AND RECREATION

Soccer is the most popular sport in Ethiopia. Many children play soccer at school and home. Ethiopia is best known for its running sports.

The Great Ethiopian Run is one of the largest races in Africa. About 46,000 runners participated in 2019! People came from around the world to race.

## ETHIOPIANS IN THE OLYMPICS

Ethiopian men and women have participated in many summer Olympic games. They have won 22 gold, 11 silver, and 21 bronze medals between 1960 and 2016. Ethiopian runner Almaz Ayana won the gold medal in the 10,000-meter dash in 2016. She completed the race in 29 minutes, 17 seconds, and broke the world record time by 14 seconds! Haile Gebrselassie is another famous runner. He has won two gold medals in long-distance running. Many people consider him to be the greatest distance runner in history.

Ethiopian gold medalist Haile Gebrselassie (right) set a record for the Great Scottish Run in 2013.

Tourists can hike the Simien Mountains to get a great view of Ethiopia.

# OUTDOOR FUN

In **rural** areas, some people play Gena. The game uses the space between two villages as boundaries. It has similar rules to field hockey.

People enjoy other outdoor activities too. Ethiopia's mountains are popular with hikers and climbers. Lake Tana and the Blue Nile are great places for sailing and rafting. From Lake Tana in the north to the Nechisar plains in the south, Ethiopia is full of natural wonders. Its unique cities, wildlife, and food make it a great place to live and visit.

## ACOOCOOLU

*Acoocoolu* is a game played by children in Ethiopia. It is similar to hide-and-seek. To play, you will need three or more people.

1. One person stands against a wall and covers his or her eyes. That person is the seeker. The seeker shouts *acoocoolu* every few seconds. This is the sound a rooster makes when the sun rises.
2. The other people hide from the seeker. If they are not ready yet, they yell *alnegam*. This means it is not morning and the seeker should not look yet.
3. Those who are hiding shout *nega* when they have hidden. This means the sun has risen.
4. The seeker tries to find them.
5. The hidden people try to sneak to the seeker's wall. They are safe if they reach the wall. But they are out if the seeker catches them before they reach it.

# GLOSSARY

**artifacts (ART-uh-fakts)** discovered objects that were made by humans

**colonizing (KOL-uh-nize-ing)** settling in a new area and taking control of it

**cultures (KUHL-churs)** the customs and ways of life for groups of people

**emperor (EM-pur-ur)** the male ruler of an area

**fossils (FOSS-uhls)** bones and other remains from ancient times

**independent (in-di-PEN-duhnt)** a country that governs itself

**native (NAY-tiv)** a person who was born in a particular country or place; also, something tied to a certain location

**rural (RUR-uhl)** the countryside

**tourists (TOOR-ists)** people who visit another country

**traditional (truh-DISH-uhn-uhl)** something handed down from one generation to another

**tropical (TROP-uh-kuhl)** a climate that is very hot and humid

# READ MORE

Brinker, Spencer. *Ethiopia*. Minneapolis, MN: Bearport Publishing, 2018.

Carruthers, Vincent. *Wildlife of Southern Africa: A Field Guide to the Animals and Plants of the Region*. Cape Town, South Africa: Struik Nature, 2016.

Hustad, Douglas. *Your Passport to Spain*. North Mankato, MN: Capstone Press, 2021.

# INTERNET SITES

**DK Find Out!: River Nile**
https://www.dkfindout.com/us/earth/rivers/river-nile

**Kids World Travel Guide: Ethiopia Facts**
https://www.kids-world-travel-guide.com/ethiopia-facts.html

**Science for Kids: Ethiopia Facts for Kids**
https://www.scienceforkidsclub.com/ethiopia-facts.html

# INDEX

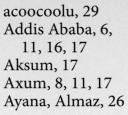

acoocoolu, 29
Addis Ababa, 6, 11, 16, 17
Aksum, 17
Axum, 8, 11, 17
Ayana, Almaz, 26

berbere, 23
Blue Nile Falls, 4, 12, 29

Christians, 8, 11, 24, 25

Danakil Desert, 14, 15

Ezana, 8

Gebrselassie, Haile, 26
Great Ethiopian Run, 26

holidays and festivals, 24–25

Italy, 10, 11, 24

Lake Tana, 12, 29
Lalibela, 16

Mercato market, 17
Mursi, 6, 21
Muslims, 8, 11, 25

Nechisar National Park, 15, 29

Omo Valley, 18, 20, 21

Selassie, Haile, 10–11

Zewde, Sahle-Work, 11

# OTHER BOOKS IN THIS SERIES

YOUR PASSPORT TO CHINA
YOUR PASSPORT TO ECUADOR
YOUR PASSPORT TO EL SALVADOR
YOUR PASSPORT TO FRANCE
YOUR PASSPORT TO IRAN
YOUR PASSPORT TO KENYA
YOUR PASSPORT TO PERU
YOUR PASSPORT TO RUSSIA
YOUR PASSPORT TO SPAIN